Go, little book, and wish to all
Flowers in the garden, meat in the hall,
A bin of wine, a spice of wit,
A house with lawns enclosing it,
A living river by the door,
A nightingale in the sycamore!

Robert Louis Stevenson

AN
ENGLISH
COTTAGE YEAR

Sally Holmes
and
Tracey Williamson

Hearst Books
New York

First published 1993

An Albion Book
Conceived, designed and produced by
The Albion Press Ltd, Spring Hill, Idbury,
Oxfordshire, England

It is the policy of William Morrow and Company, Inc., and its imprints and
affiliates, recognizing the importance of preserving what has been written,
to print the books we publish on acid-free paper, and we exert our best
efforts to that end.

Library-of-Congress Cataloging-in-Publication Data
An English cottage year / [compiled by] Sally Holmes. -- 1st ed.
p. cm.
ISBN 0-688-11965-4 : $17.00
I. Holmes, Sally.
PN6071.S4114E54 1993
820.8'033--dc20
93-1506 CIP
Printed in Italy by New Interlitho

First edition

1   2   3   4   5   6   7   8   9   10

CONTENTS

Oh! yet
Stands the church clock at ten to three?
And is there honey still for tea?

Rupert Brooke

SPRING

Birds' love and birds' song
    Flying here and there,
Birds' song and birds' love,
    And you with gold for hair!
Birds' song and birds' love,
    Passing with the weather,
Men's song and men's love,
    To love once and for ever.

Men's love and birds' love,
    And women's love and men's!
And you my wren with a crown of gold,
    And you my queen of the wrens!
You the queen of the wrens –
    We'll be birds of a feather,
I'll be King of the Queen of the wrens,
    And all in a nest together.

Alfred, Lord Tennyson

Spring, when the earth wakes from its winter sleep, is the time of renewal, when we should all be, in the words of William Blake, "as happy as birds in the spring."

The air is soft. Violets blow. Snow lies under hedges. Men plow.

Gilbert White

It is not spring until you can plant your foot upon twelve daisies.

Traditional

The miracle of rising yeast is a spring in miniature.

14

AN ENGLISH LOAF

1 ½ lb/675 g strong (all-purpose) white flour
½ oz/15 g fresh yeast (or the equivalent amount of dried yeast)
¾ pt/450 ml warm water
¾ oz/20 g sea salt

Cream the yeast with a little of the water and dissolve the salt in the rest of the water. Put the flour in a large bowl, make a well in the centre and pour in the creamed yeast. Give a quick stir to mix the yeast with the flour, pour in the salty water and stir again to combine all the ingredients. Then knead the dough with your hands (if at any stage it feels too sticky to work, sprinkle over a little more flour). After a few minutes' kneading the dough will feel smooth and springy and come away cleanly from the sides of the bowl. Form the dough into a ball, cover it with a cloth and leave it in a warm place to rise.

In 3 hours or so, the dough will have doubled its volume. Knead it again for 3 or 4 minutes, transfer it to a greased 2¼ lb/1 kg loaf tin and leave it to rise for a second time. After about 2 hours, when the dough has risen just above the top of the tin, heat the oven to 200°C/400°F/gas mark 6. Put the loaf into the hot oven and bake for 40 minutes. Take it from the tin and, to test whether it is cooked, tap it on the bottom. It should sound hollow. If it has a dull sound, put it back in the oven for 5 minutes, then test again. Leave the loaf to cool on a rack, or lying across the empty tin.

Now infant April joins the spring,
    And views the watery sky,
As youngling linnet tries its wing,
    And fears at first to fly;
With timid steps she ventures on,
    And hardly dares to smile,
Till blossoms open one by one,
    And sunny hours beguile.

But finer days are coming yet,
    With scenes more sweet to charm,
And suns arrive that rise and set
    Bright strangers to a storm:
Then, as the birds with louder song
    Each morning's glory cheer,
With bolder step she speeds along,
    And loses all her fear.

In wanton gambols, like a child,
    She tends her early toils,
And seeks the buds along the wild,
    That blossoms while she smiles;
Or, laughing on, with naught to chide,
    She races with the Hours,
Or sports by Nature's lovely side,
    And fills her lap with flowers.

John Clare

16

Rose not till half past eight. A heavenly morning. As soon as breakfast was over we went into the garden and sowed the scarlet beans about the house. It was a clear sky a heavenly morning. I sowed the flowers, William helped me. We then went and sat in the orchard till dinner time. It was very hot. William wrote "The Celandine." We planned a shed for the sun was too much for us.

Dorothy Wordsworth

Pansies, lilies, kingcups, daisies,
Let them live upon their praises;
Long as there's a sun that sets,
Primroses will have their glory;
Long as there are violets,
They will have a place in story:
There's a flower that shall be mine,
'Tis the little celandine.

William Wordsworth

The cuckoo's a bonny bird, he whistles as he flies,
He brings us good tidings, he tells us no lies;
He sucks little birds' eggs to make his voice clear,
And never sings cuckoo till summer is near.
Sing cuckoo in April, cuckoo in May,
Cuckoo in June, and then flies away.

Traditional

When green buds hang in the elm like dust
    And sprinkle the lime like rain,
Forth I wander, forth I must,
    And drink of life again.
Forth I must by hedgerow bowers
    To look at the leaves uncurled,
And stand in the fields where cuckoo-flowers
    Are lying about the world.

A.E. Housman

18

Oh, to be in England
Now that April's there,
And whoever wakes in England
Sees, some morning, unaware,
That the lowest boughs and the brushwood sheaf
Round the elm-tree bole are in tiny leaf,
While the chaffinch sings on the orchard bough
In England – now!

Robert Browning

Who loves a garden loves a greenhouse too.

William Cowper

This rule in gardening never forget,
To sow dry and plant wet.

Traditional

One for the mouse and one for the crow,
One to rot and one to grow.

Traditional

Plant your sage and rue together,
The sage will grow in any weather.

Traditional

SOWING

It was a perfect day
For sowing; just
As sweet and dry was the ground
As tobacco-dust.

I tasted deep the hour
Between the far
Owl's chuckling first soft cry
And the first star.

A long stretched hour it was;
Nothing undone
Remained; the early seeds
All safely sown.

And now, hark at the rain,
Windless and light,
Half a kiss, half a tear,
Saying good-night.

Edward Thomas

GOD'S ACRE

Hail, garden of confident hope!
    Where sweet seeds are quickening in darkness and cold;
        For how sweet and how young they will be
    When they pierce thro' the mould.
Balm, myrtle and heliotrope
    There watch and there wait out of sight for their Sun:
        While the Sun, which they see not, doth see
Each and all one by one.

Christina Rossetti

It was traditional to plant seeds on Good Friday, although sweet peas were planted on St. Patrick's day, 17th March. As a general rule, seeds should always be planted under a waxing, not a waning, moon.

Eggs, the symbol of rebirth, have always had a special importance at Easter, and painted or dyed eggs are the only decoration an Easter table needs. An Easter egg hunt in the garden for tiny chocolate eggs hidden by the Easter hare is a more recent, but equally welcome custom.

At Easter we eat hot cross buns which, if made on Good Friday itself, were long considered to have protective and healing powers. Sailors would take them to sea, and farmers left them in their granaries to ward off rats. The history of the buns stretches back to the wheaten cakes eaten at pagan spring festivals, made holy by the cross.

Hot cross buns! Hot cross buns!
One a penny, two a penny,
Hot cross buns!

Traditional

Easter was one of the times in the English countryside when the labourers and their children would tour the villages entreating in traditional rhyme for money or beer. The "pace-eggers" would sing:

Here's two or three jolly boys
All of one mind,
We've come a pace-egging,
And hope you'll be kind;
We hope you'll be kind
With your eggs and your beer,
And we'll come no more pace-egging
Until the next year.

Traditional

English countryfolk used to rise early on Easter Sunday to see the sun dance for joy.

To create a little flower is the labour of ages.

William Blake

I always think it desirable to group together flowers that bloom at the same time. It is impossible, even undesirable, to have a garden in blossom all over, and groups of flower-beauty are all the more enjoyable for being more or less isolated by stretches of intervening greenery.

Gertrude Jekyll

A sweet morning. We have put the finishing stroke to our bower and here we are sitting in the orchard. It is one o'clock. We are sitting upon a seat under the wall which I found my brother building up when I came to him with his apple – he had intended that it should have been done before I came. It is a nice cool shady spot. The small birds are singing, lambs bleating, cuckoo calling. The thrush sings by fits. Thomas Ashburner's axe is going quietly (without passion) in the orchard. Hens are cackling, flies humming, the women talking together at their doors: plum and peach trees are in blossom – apple trees greenish – the opposite woods green, the crows are cawing. We have heard ravens. The ash trees are in blossom, birds flying all about us.

Dorothy Wordsworth

A real May-day at last; warm, west wind, sunshine; birds singing as if hearts would burst; four or five blackbirds all in hearing at once; butterfly, small white, tipped with yellowish red; song of thrush more varied even than nightingale; if rare, people would go miles to hear it, never the same in same bird, and every bird different; fearless, too; *operatic* singer.

Richard Jefferies

Good morning, ladies and gentlemen, it is the first of May,
And we are come to garlanding because it is new May Day;
A bunch of flowers we have brought you, and at your door we
    stay,
So please to give us what you can, and then we'll go away.

Traditional

SUMMER

Come, cuckoo, come:
Come again, swift swallow:
Come and welcome! when you come
Summer's sure to follow:
June the month of months
Flowers and fruitage brings too,
When green trees spread shadiest boughs,
When each wild bird sings too.

If the year would stand
Still at June for ever,
With no further growth on land
Nor further flow of river,
If all nights were shortest nights
And longest days were all the seven,
This might be a merrier world
To my mind to live in.

Christina Rossetti

29

Summer afternoon — summer afternoon; to me those have always been the two most beautiful words in the English language.

Henry James

It was between the may and the June roses. The may bloom had fallen, and among the hawthorn boughs were the little green bunches that would feed the redwings in autumn. High up the briars had climbed, straight and towering while there was a thorn or an ash sapling, or a yellow-green willow, to uphold them, and then curving over towards the meadow. The buds were on them, but not yet open; it was between the may and the rose.

Richard Jefferies

Gather ye rosebuds while ye may.

Robert Herrick

HONEY AND OAT BARS

4 oz/100 g butter or margarine   2 tablespoons runny honey
4 oz/100 g Demerara sugar   8 oz/225 g rolled oats

Preheat the oven to 180°C/350°F/gas mark 4. Grease an 7 × 10 inch/18 × 25 cm shallow baking tin. Melt the butter or margarine in a saucepan. Add the sugar and the honey, cook for 1 minute, take off the heat and mix in the oats.

Press the mixture into the baking tin, leaving a small amount of room for expansion around the edges. Bake for about 15 to 20 minutes, until golden brown. Cut into bars while still warm; take out of the tin when cold. Store in an airtight container.

The custom of "telling the bees" about any great event in the family was known all over England. It was felt especially important to tell bees of the death of the master of the house, and entreat them to remain. The bee-hive would be draped in mourning, and the bees would be solemnly addressed in rhyme, such as:

> Honey bees! Honey bees, hear what I say!
> Your master has passed away.
> But his wife now begs you will freely stay,
> And still gather honey for many a day.
> Bonny bees, bonny bees, hear what I say!

THE SEEDS OF LOVE

I sowed three seeds of love,
    And I sowed them in the spring,
In April, May, and June likewise,
    When the small birds so sweetly sing.

My garden was well planted
    With flowers everywhere,
But I had not the liberty of choosing for myself
    The flower I loved so dear.

My gardener was standing by,
    I asked him to choose for me,
He chose me the violet, the lily, and the pink,
    And it's them I refused all three.

The violet I did not like,
    Because it does fade away so soon,
And the lily and the pink I did overlook,
    I resolved to tarry till June.

In June there's a red rosebud,
  And that is the flower for me;
I ofttimes plucked at the red rosebud
  Till I gainéd the willow tree.

The willow tree will twist,
  And the willow tree will twine,
And I wish I was in the young man's arms
  That stole away this heart of mine.

Then a bunch of rue I'll wear,
  That no one can ever touch,
And I'll let the world so plainly see
  That I loved one flower too much.

Traditional

A beautiful peaceful summer Sunday morn such as Robert Burns would have loved. Perfect peace and rest. The sun and the golden buttercup meadows had it almost to themselves. A few soft fleecy clouds were rising out of the west but the gentle warm air scarcely stirred even the leaves on the lofty tops of the great poplars. One or two people were crossing the Common early by the several paths through the golden sea of buttercups which will soon be the silver sea of ox-eyes. The birds were singing quietly. The cuckoo's notes tolled clear and sweet as a silver bell.

Francis Kilvert

I value my garden more for being full of blackbirds than of cherries, and very frankly give them fruit for their songs.

Joseph Addison

Flower in the crannied wall,
I pluck you out of the crannies,
I hold you here, root and all, in my hand,
Little flower – but *if* I could understand
What you are, root and all, and all in all,
I should know what God and man is.

Alfred, Lord Tennyson

Afternoon tea, preferably taken outdoors beneath a tree, is one of the most enduring of cottage pleasures, as Henry James records:

Under certain circumstances there are few hours in life more agreeable than the hour dedicated to the ceremony known as afternoon tea. There are circumstances in which, whether you partake of the tea or not – some people of course never do, – the situation is in itself delightful.

The implements of the little feast had been disposed upon the lawn of an old English country-house, in what I should call the perfect middle of a splendid summer afternoon. Part of the afternoon had waned, but much of what was left was of the finest and rarest quality. Real dusk would not arrive for many hours; but the flood of summer light had begun to ebb, the air had grown mellow, the shadows were long upon the smooth, dense turf. They lengthened slowly, however, and the scene expressed that sense of leisure still to come which is perhaps the chief source of one's enjoyment of such a scene at such an hour. From five o'clock to eight is on certain occasions a little eternity; but on such an occasion as this the interval could only be an eternity of pleasure.

Henry James

In the country I always fear that creation will expire before tea-time.

Sydney Smith

Of course not every summer's day is as blissful as this. English summer weather can justify Samuel Taylor Coleridge's gloomy comment that, "Summer has set in with its usual severity." But summer rain is the gardener's friend.

Weeding is a delightful occupation, especially after summer rain, when the roots come up clear and clean. One gets to know how many and various are the ways of weeds – as many almost as the moods of human creatures. How easy and pleasant to pull up are the soft annuals like Chickweed and Groundsel, and how one looks with respect at deep-rooted things like Docks, that make one go and fetch a spade.

Gertrude Jekyll

One year's seeding means seven years' weeding.

Traditional

THE RAIN

I hear leaves drinking rain;
    I hear rich leaves on top
Giving the poor beneath
    Drop after drop;
'Tis a sweet noise to hear
These green leaves drinking near.

And when the Sun comes out,
    After this rain shall stop
A wondrous light will fill
    Each dark, round drop;
I hope the Sun shines bright;
'Twill be a lovely sight.

W.H. Davies

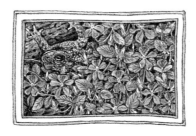

PEA SOUP

1 lb/450 g green peas
½ oz/12 g butter
1 onion, thinly sliced
Handful of mint or parsley
1 pt/600 ml chicken or vegetable stock

salt and pepper
2 teaspoons flour
4 tablespoons milk
1 tablespoon double cream

First, shell the peas. Melt the butter in a pan and cook the onion until it is transparent. Stir peas into the butter and onion mixture. Add the mint or parsley, stock, salt and pepper and simmer for 30 minutes. Purée the soup and then thicken with blended flour and milk, season to taste and decorate with a swirl of cream.

I have learned much from the little cottage gardens that help to make our English waysides the prettiest in the temperate world. One can hardly go into the smallest cottage garden without learning or observing something new. It may be some two plants growing beautifully together by some happy chance, or a pretty mixed tangle of creepers, or something that one always thought must have a south wall doing better on an east one. But eye and brain must be alert to receive the impression and studious to store it, to add to the hoard of experience. And it is important to train oneself to have a good flower-eye; to be able to see at a glance what flowers are good and which are unworthy, and why, and to keep an open mind about it; not to be swayed by the petty tyrannies of the "florist" or show judge; for, though some part of his judgment may be sound, he is himself a slave to rules, and must go by points which are defined arbitrarily and rigidly, and have reference mainly to the show table, leaving out of account, as if unworthy of consideration, such matters as gardens and garden beauty, and human delight, and sunshine, and varying lights of morning and evening and noonday.

Gertrude Jekyll

HOW TO TRIM A HAT

Trimming a hat for a special occasion is always fun. Go into the garden and gather a handful of leaves and flowers with longish stems. Choose flowers which are not quite open. Take a straw hat and bind the leaves and flowers around the base of the crown and attach with either florist's wire or ribbon. If it is a blowy day attach two ribbons to the sides of the hat and tie under the chin.

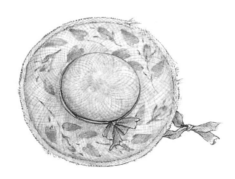

POTPOURRI

A way to make your whole house smell fresh is to gather your own potpourri of petals and flower heads and dry them in your airing cupboard. To revive tired potpourri, sprinkle with rose-water.

LAVENDER BAGS

Cut lavender heads when they are fully out and then dry out on newspaper or on a tray in the airing cupboard for several weeks. From muslin or thin cotton lawn make little bags about 2 ½ inch/65 mm square and sew round three sides putting right sides of material together. Turn bags inside out to leave stitching on the inside and cut the top with pinking shears to stop the edges fraying. Two-thirds fill the bags with the dried lavender and tie up the tops tightly with a narrow satin ribbon. Lavender bags make perfect little gifts to bring freshness and country fragrance to clothes drawers.

To gather fruit for jam is one of life's simplest and fullest pleasures. As Jane Austen's characters agree in a memorable strawberry-gathering scene in Emma, to pick the fruits oneself is "the only way of really enjoying them."

Generally speaking, jam is easily made by boiling together fruit and sugar with some lemon juice and perhaps some water. Here are some tips: If you leave strawberries in their own weight of sugar in a covered bowl overnight, the sugar draws out the juice making the berries firmer so that they stay whole when cooked; apricot jam is marvellously improved by the addition of blanched, split almonds.

GOOSEBERRY AND ELDERFLOWER JAM

3 lb/1.25 kg gooseberries,
  topped, tailed and washed
5 or 6 elderflower heads

2 pints/1.25 litres water
4 lb/1.75 kg sugar
Makes about 6 lb/2.75 kg

(You will also need a piece of muslin at least 10 inches/25 cm square and some string.)

Tie up the elderflowers in the piece of muslin. Put them in a preserving pan with the gooseberries and the water and simmer for about 30 minutes, till the gooseberries are soft and the contents of the pan are reduced by about a third. Meanwhile, warm the sugar for 15 minutes in a moderate oven (180°C/350°F/gas mark 4). Take out the elderflowers, stir in the warmed sugar and cook slowly, stirring often, till the sugar has dissolved. Turn up the heat and boil hard, stirring from time to time, for 15 minutes. Test for setting. If necessary, continue to boil and test till setting point is reached. Remove any froth from the surface. Leave the jam to settle for 15 minutes, ladle it into hot sterilized jars, cover and refrigerate when cool. Use quickly.

Summer is the time for picnics, and every picnic has its own magic, though none can ever quite match up to the glorious feast enjoyed by Mole and Rat as they mess about in a boat at the beginning of that idyll to the English countryside, The Wind in the Willows:

The Mole waggled his toes from sheer happiness, spread his chest with a sigh of full contentment, and leaned back blissfully into the soft cushions. "*What* a day I'm having!" he said. "Let us start at once!"

"Hold hard a minute, then!" said the Rat. He looped the painter through a ring in his landing-stage, climbed up into his hole above, and after a short interval reappeared staggering under a fat, wicker luncheon-basket.

"Shove that under your feet," he observed to the Mole, as he passed it down into the boat. Then he untied the painter and took the sculls again.

"What's inside it?" asked the Mole, wriggling with curiosity.

"There's cold chicken inside it," replied the Rat briefly; "coldtonguecoldhamcoldbeefpickledgherkinssaladfrenchrolls cresssandwichesspottedmeatgingerbeerlemonadesodawater – "

"O stop, stop," cried the Mole in ecstasies: "This is too much!"

"Do you really think so?" inquired the Rat seriously. "It's only what I always take on these little excursions; and the other animals are always telling me that I'm a mean beast and cut it *very* fine!"

Kenneth Grahame

48

Here's a health to the world, as round as a wheel,
Death is a thing we all shall feel;
If life were a thing that money could buy
The rich would live and the poor would die.

Traditional

Here's to the inside of a loaf and the outside of a gaol,
A good beefsteak and a quart of good ale.

Traditional

A GREEN SALAD

For the salad
½ fresh lettuce
½ cos lettuce
½ bunch salad onions
1 large handful watercress
Several sorrel leaves

For the vinaigrette dressing
1 tablespoon French mustard
2 lemons, strained juice
2 fl oz/60 ml white wine vinegar
1 teaspoon salt
Pepper to taste
½ pt/300 ml sunflower oil
¼ pt/150 ml virgin olive oil

Wash and dry all the leaves and salad onions thoroughly. Tear them into small pieces and put them in a salad bowl.

To make the dressing, put the mustard in a small bowl and whisk in the lemon juice and the wine vinegar, and then the salt and pepper. Slowly beat in the sunflower oil, poured in a thin stream, and follow this with the olive oil. When thoroughly mixed, pour into a jug and serve with the leaves.

50

BABY TOMATOES WITH TWO STUFFINGS

20 cherry tomatoes	6 oz/175 g tuna
3 stalks celery, finely chopped	1 ½ tablespoons mayonnaise
3 oz/75 g cream cheese	1 ½ tablespoons chopped
2 teaspoons lemon juice	parsley
Salt and pepper	Salt and pepper

Wash and dry the tomatoes and remove the stalks. Cut a little slice off the bottom of each one so that they stand upright, then slice off the tops cleanly. Use a small coffee spoon to scrape out the seeds and the pulp. Place the tomato shells upside down on a draining board or a small mesh rack and allow them to drain for about an hour. Then store them upside down in the fridge till you are ready to stuff them.

Mix the chopped celery with the cream cheese and 1 teaspoon of the lemon juice. Season with salt and pepper to taste and use to fill half the tomatoes.

Mix the tuna with the mayonnaise, the parsley and the other teaspoon of lemon juice. Mash with a fork into a paste, and season with salt and pepper. Spoon the mixture into the remaining 10 tomatoes.

Who loves a garden loves a greenhouse too.

William Cowper

He that would eat fruit must climb the tree.

Traditional

'Tis the last rose of summer
Left blooming alone;
All her lovely companions
Are faded and gone.

Thomas Moore

Summer's lease hath all too short a date.

William Shakespeare

AUTUMN

Season of mists and mellow fruitfulness!
　　Close bosom-friend of the maturing sun;
Conspiring with him to lead and bless
　　With fruit the vines that round the thatch-eaves run;
To bend with apples the moss'd cottage-trees,
　　And fill all fruit with ripeness to the core;
　　　　To swell the gourd, and plump the hazel shells
　　With a sweet kernel; to set budding more
And still more, later flowers for the bees,
Until they think warm days will never cease;
　　　　For summer has o'er-brimmed their clammy cells.

John Keats

Country writer Richard Jefferies gives the best description of the cramped profusion of the nineteenth-century cottage garden:

Trees fill up every available space and corner – apple trees, pear trees, damsons, plums, bullaces – all varieties. The cottagers seem to like to have at least one tree of every sort. These trees look very nice in the spring when the apple blossom is out, and again in the autumn when the fruit is ripe. Under the trees are gooseberry bushes, raspberries, and numbers of currants. The patches are divided into strips producing potatoes, cabbage, lettuce, onions, radishes, parsnips; in this kitchen produce, as with the fruit, they like to possess a few of all kinds. There is generally a great bunch of rhubarb.

I do not envy the owners of very large gardens. The garden should fit its master or his tastes just as his clothes do; it should be neither too large nor too small, but just comfortable. If the garden is larger than he can individually govern and plan and look after, then he is no longer its master but its slave, just as surely as the much-too-rich man is the slave and not the master of his superfluous wealth.

Gertrude Jekyll

A camomile bed,
The more it is trodden,
The more it will spread.

Traditional

GREEN TOMATO CHUTNEY

4 lb/1.8 kg green tomatoes
1 lb/450 g cooking apples
½ lb/225 g stoned raisins
1 lb/450 g brown sugar
6 medium onions

12 red chillies or a tablespoon of
   pickling spices tied up in muslin
1 dessertspoon salt
1 pt/600 ml wine vinegar

Chop the tomatoes and apples and put them in a large pan. Add the raisins, brown sugar, chopped onions, muslin bag of chillies or spices, salt and vinegar. Simmer until thick. Remove the spices and pot up the chutney in hot, sterilized jars. Cover each jar with a circle of greaseproof paper and refrigerate when cool. Use quickly.

Makes approximately 8 jars.

LEMON CURD

juice and thinly pared rind of
  6 large lemons
12 oz/350 g butter, cut in little
  pieces

2 lb/900 g caster (superfine)
  sugar
8 eggs, beaten
Makes about 3 lb/1.25 kg

Lemon curd is very easy to make, as long as the heat is kept low. The mixture must not come to the boil, or it will curdle.

Put all the ingredients in a bowl set over a saucepan of simmering water, or in the top of a double boiler. Cook, stirring, till the butter has melted and the sugar has completely dissolved. Take the bowl from the heat and strain the mixture through a nylon sieve into another bowl. Discard the lemon rind. Put the strained mixture, in a clean bowl, back on top of the pan of hot water or pour it into the cleaned top of the double boiler. Continue to cook, stirring frequently, till the curd is thick enough to coat the back of a wooden spoon. This may take 40 minutes, or even longer.

Ladle the curd into hot, sterilized jars. Cover the surface of the curd in each jar with a waxed paper disc, then cover the jars. Label them when they are cold and refrigerate. Use quickly.

Lemon curd is delicious used as a spread, as a filling for tarts or to sandwich the two halves of a sponge cake. Orange curd makes a pleasant and more unusual alternative.

My occupation is, writing another tragedy — my amusement is, gardening. I have now in my little garden one of the most beautiful chrysanthemums ever seen . . . It is a very large double white flower, almost as pure and splendid as the double white camelia, and has in the inside a spot larger than a shilling of the deepest, richest, purple. You never saw anything more magnificent. We imagine that this extraordinary colouring must have proceeded from some of the purple plant being mixed in with the root of the white, which is in itself a very beautiful contrast; but the white, with the purple inside, is really superb. It is covered with blossoms, and excites the envy of all the gardeners and half the ladies in the neighbourhood.

Mary Russell Mitford

The sky this evening, being what they call a mackerel sky, was most beautiful, & much admired in many parts of the country. As the beautiful mackerel sky was remarked & admired at Ringmer, near Lewes, London, & Selbourne at the same time, it is a plain proof that those fleecy clouds were very high in the atmosphere.

Gilbert White

A mackerel sky,
Never holds three days dry.

Traditional

Here's to the old apple tree,
Bud and blow,
And bear apples enow,
Hats-full, caps-full, three-bushel bags-full
And some for the boys to steal.

Traditional

Stolen fruit is sweet.

Traditional

SHORTENING DAYS AT THE HOMESTEAD

The first fire since the summer is lit, and is smoking into the
room:
      The sun-rays thread it through, like woof-lines in a
        loom.
      Sparrows spurt from the hedge, whom misgivings appal
That winter did not leave last year for ever, after all.
      Like shock-headed urchins, spiny-haired,
      Stand pollard windows, their twigs just bared.

Who is this coming with pondering pace,
Black and ruddy, with white embossed,
His eyes being black, and ruddy his face,
And the marge of his hair like morning frost?
      It's the cider-maker,
      And appletree-shaker,
And behind him on wheels, in readiness,
His mill, and tubs, and vat, and press.

Thomas Hardy

63

Nothing I like better than a baked apple.

Jane Austen, Emma

I'd rather have a young man with an apple in his hand,
Than I would have an old man with houses and with land;
For an old man he comes grumping in, always full of care,
But a young man comes in whistling with, "How do, my dear?"

Traditional

Stay me with flagons, comfort me with apples: for I am sick
of love.

The Song of Solomon

The best things in life are free.

Traditional

I love the fitful gust that shakes
    The casement all the day,
And from the mossy elm-tree takes
    The faded leaf away,
Twirling it by the window pane
With thousand others down the lane.

I love to see the cottage smoke
    Curl upwards through the trees,
The pigeons nestled round the cote
    On November days like these;
The cock upon the dunghill crowing,
The mill-sails on the heath a-going.

John Clare

Today I think
Only with scents, – scents dead leaves yield,
And bracken, and wild carrot's seed,
And the square mustard field;

Odours that rise
When the spade wounds the roots of tree,
Rose, currant, raspberry, or goutweed,
Rhubarb or celery;

The smoke's smell, too,
Flowing from where a bonfire burns
The dead, the waste, the dangerous,
And all to sweetness turns.

It is enough
To smell, to crumble the dark earth,
While the robin sings over again
Sad songs of Autumn mirth.

Edward Thomas

Oh, good gigantic smile o' the brown old earth,
This autumn morning!

Robert Browning

The autumn's wind on suthering wings
Plays round the oak-tree strong
And through the hawthorn hedges sings
The year's departing song.
There's every leaf upon the whirl
Ten thousand times an hour,
The grassy meadows crisp and curl
With here and there a flower.
There's nothing in this world I find
But wakens to the autumn wind.

John Clare

At Halloween, October 31st, witches, fairies, and ghosts are abroad. It is a time for fun and mischief, with traditional games such as bobbing for apples in a tub of water: contestants must have their hands tied behind their backs and remove the apples with their teeth. It is the last day of the old Celtic year, when the pagan Celts would light ritual hilltop fires at dusk. Because of its magical associations, Halloween has always been a popular night for divination. Here, from the folklorist S. O. Addy, are three methods of finding out who you will marry:

On Halloween people go out in the dark and pluck cabbage-stalks. If on this eve you scatter seeds or ashes down a lane, and a girl follows you in the direction in which you have gone, she will be your wife.

If you eat an apple at midnight upon All Halloween, and, without looking behind you, gaze into a mirror, you will see the face of your future husband or wife.

On Hallows Eve let a girl cross her shoes upon her bedroom floor in the shape of a T and say these lines:

> *I cross my shoes in the shape of a T,*
> *Hoping this night my true love to see,*
> *Not in his best or worst array,*
> *But in the clothes of every day.*

Then let her get into bed backwards without speaking any more that night, when she will see her future husband in her dreams.

Hey-how for Halloween!
All the witches to be seen,
Some black and some green,
Hey-how for Halloween!

Traditional

From ghoulies and ghosties and long-leggety beasties
And things that go bump in the night,
Good Lord, deliver us!

Traditional

Autumn is, as the poet Laurence Binyon wrote in a moving poem after the First World War, "the time for the burning of the leaves." And what better way to do so than in a Guy Fawkes bonfire on November 5th, burning in effigy the conspirator with whose thwarted attempt to blow up the Houses of Parliament every British citizen feels a sneaking sympathy?

Please to remember the Fifth of November,
Gunpowder, treason and plot.
We know no reason why gunpowder treason
Should ever be forgot.

Traditional

Bonfire night, the stars are bright,
Every little angel dressed in white.
Can you eat a biscuit?
Can you smoke a pipe?
Can you go a-courting
At ten o'clock at night?

Traditional

Onion's skin very thin,
Mild winter coming in;
Onion's skin thick and tough,
Coming winter cold and rough

Traditional

If there's ice in November that'll bear a duck,
There'll be nothing after but sludge and muck.

Traditional

WINTER

The frost is here,
And fuel is dear,
And woods are sear,
And fires burn clear,
And frost is here
And has bitten the heel of the going year.

Bite, frost, bite!
You roll up away from the light
The blue wood-louse, and the plump dormouse,
And the bees are still'd, and the flies are kill'd,
And you bite far into the heart of the house,
But not into mine.

Bite, frost, bite!
The woods are all the searer,
The fuel is all the dearer,
The fires are all the clearer,
My spring is all the nearer,
You have bitten into the heart of the earth,
But not into mine.

Alfred, Lord Tennyson

Lord Byron defined the English winter as "ending in July, to recommence in August." For all the beauties of the winter landscape, it certainly can seem long drawn-out; we can all agree with Addison's Sir Roger de Coverley in his observation that, "it happens very well that Christmas should fall out in the Middle of Winter." Christmas is, of course, largely a re-definition of the pagan midwinter festivals it replaced, and many of whose traditions it adapted. Most of today's traditions centre on present-giving, eating, or drinking: preferably all three at once. The cottage Christmas especially calls out for home-made treats, such as mince pies made with Mrs. Griggs's Mincemeat.

MRS GRIGGS'S MINCEMEAT

12 oz/350 g sultanas

12 oz/350 g raisins

12 oz/350 g currants

8 oz/225 g chopped mixed peel

8 oz/225 g almonds, blanched
and slivered

8 oz/225 g cooking apples,
peeled, cored and grated

8 oz/225 g Barbados or
Demerara sugar

8 oz/225 g beef suet, finely
chopped

1 teaspoon ground cinnamon

1 teaspoon grated nutmeg

2 teaspoons ground mixed spice

juice and finely grated rind of
1 large lemon

juice and finely grated rind of
1 medium orange

¼ pint/150 ml brandy

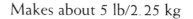

Makes about 5 lb/2.25 kg

Put all the ingredients except the fruit juice and brandy in a
large bowl and mix them together very thoroughly. Stir in
the fruit juice and then the brandy, then spoon the mixture
into hot, sterilized jars. Cover the surface of the mincemeat
in each jar with a waxed paper disc, then cover and label the
jars. Store the mincemeat in the refrigerator. It should be
allowed to mature for 4 weeks before it is used. If it becomes
dry during storage, stir in a little more brandy. Serve with
brandy butter.

O thought I!
What a beautiful thing
God has made winter to be
by stripping the trees
and letting us see
their shapes and forms.
What a freedom does it seem
to give to the storms.

Dorothy Wordsworth

There is a beauty in trees peculiar to winter, when their fair delicate slender tracery unveiled by leaves and showing clearly against the sky rises bending with a lofty arch or sweeps gracefully drooping. The crossing and interlacing of the limbs, the smaller boughs and tender twigs make an exquisitely fine network which has something of the severe beauty of sculpture, while the tree in summer in its full pride and splendour and colour of foliage represents the loveliness of painting. The deciduous trees which seem to me most graceful and elegant in winter are the birches, limes, beeches.

Francis Kilvert

MULLED WINE

2 ½ pints/1.5 litres red wine
about 10 lumps sugar
1 Seville orange
1 lemon
6 cloves
2 inch/5 cm stick of cinnamon

1 teaspoon ground ginger
1 bay leaf
about 4 fl oz/125 ml brandy
   (optional)

Makes about 2½ pints (1.5 litres)

Rub the sugar lumps over the orange and the lemon to release their zest, and put the sugar in a large pan. Stick the orange with the cloves and add it to the pan. Squeeze the juice from half the lemon, strain it and pour it in; cut the other half into thin slices and add them. Put the cinnamon, ginger and the torn bay leaf into the pan and pour in the red wine.

Set the pan over a low heat until the wine is just simmering and a scum has formed on the surface. Take the pan off the heat and remove the scum with a metal spoon. Strain the mulled wine into a clean pan and, if you like, add the brandy. Serve it in heatproof glasses, decorated with fresh, thin slices of orange and lemon.

Reheat the mulled wine as necessary, slowly over a low heat; do not let it boil.

In the New Forest, villagers used to pour libations of spiced ale in the orchards and meadows on Christmas Eve, singing:

> Apples and pears without good corn,
> Come in plenty to every one;
> Eat and drink good cakes and hot ale,
> Give earth to drink and she'll not fail.

Of course, it's not necessary, having mulled your ale or wine, to throw it away . . .

If it were possible to simplify life to the utmost, how little one really wants! And is it a blessing or a disadvantage to be so made that one *must* take keen interest in many matters; that, seeing something one's hand may do, one cannot resist doing or attempting it, even though time be already over-crowded, and strength much reduced, and sight steadily failing? Are the people happier who are content to drift comfortably down the stream of life, to take things easily, not to *want* to take pains or give themselves trouble about what is not exactly necessary? I know not which, as worldly wisdom, is the wiser; I only know that to my own mind and conscience pure idleness seems to me akin to folly, or even worse, and that in some form or other I must obey the Divine command: "Work while ye have the light."

Gertrude Jekyll

Summer fading, winter comes —
Frosty mornings, tingling thumbs,
Window robins, winter rooks,
And the picture story-books.

Robert Louis Stevenson

YULE LOG

2 oz/50 g plain flour
1 oz/25 g cocoa powder
3 medium eggs
4 oz/100 g caster (superfine)
  sugar
1 tablespoon warm water
Filling
8 oz/250 g sweetened chestnut
  purée

½ pint/300 ml double cream,
  whipped
Topping
4 oz/100 g chocolate butter cream
1 tablespoon icing (confectioners')
  sugar

Makes an 8 inch/20 cm log

Preheat the oven to 200°C/400°F/gas mark 6. Grease an 8 × 12 inch/20 × 30 cm Swiss roll tin and line it with non-stick baking parchment or buttered greaseproof paper.

Sieve the flour with the cocoa. Using a balloon whisk or an electric beater, whisk the eggs and the sugar together till the mixture is pale and thick. Fold the flour mixture into the eggs, then fold in the water. Pour the mixture into the tin and bake the sponge for about 10 minutes, till it feels springy.

While the cake is baking, spread a damp cloth on a work surface. Lay a sheet of greaseproof paper on top and sprinkle the paper with caster (superfine) sugar. As soon as you take the sponge from the oven, run a knife round the edges to loosen it, and turn it out on to the paper. Peel away the lining paper and trim off the crisp edges of the cake. Cover the sponge with another piece of greaseproof paper. To make it easier to start rolling, cut almost through one short side of the sponge, about 1 inch/2.5 cm in from the edge. Lift the ends of the cloth and use it to roll up the sponge round the top sheet of paper. Cover the cake with the damp cloth, and leave it to cool.

When the sponge is quite cold, unroll it and remove the top piece of paper. Spread a layer of chestnut purée, followed by a layer of whipped cream, all over the inner surface and carefully roll it up again. Set the roll on a plate, with the join underneath. Spread chocolate butter cream over the outside of the roll. With the tip of a knife, swirl a spiral in the butter cream on each end of the log. Drag the prongs of a fork along the length of the cake, to create an effect of tree bark, and sieve the icing sugar over the top, for snow. If you like, complete the decoration of the yule log with a piece of holly.

THE OXEN

Christmas Eve, and twelve of the clock.
    "Now they are all on their knees,"
An elder said as we sat in a flock
    By the embers in hearthside ease.

We pictured the meek mild creatures where
    They dwelt in a strawy pen,
Nor did it occur to one of us there
    To doubt they were kneeling then.

So fair a fancy few would weave
    In these years! Yet, I feel,
If someone said on Christmas Eve,
    "Come; see the oxen kneel

"In the lonely barton by yonder coomb
    Our childhood used to know,"
I should go with him in the gloom,
    Hoping it might be so.

Thomas Hardy

Speaking of the blowing of the Holy Thorn and the kneeling and weeping of the oxen on old Christmas Eve (tonight) Priscilla said, "I have known James Meredith 40 years and I have never known him far from the truth, and I said to him one day, 'James, tell me the truth, did you ever see the oxen kneel on old Christmas Eve at the Weston?' And he said, 'No, I never saw them kneel at the Weston but when I was at Hinton at Staunton-on-Wye I saw them. I was watching them on old Christmas Eve and at 12 o'clock the oxen that were standing knelt down upon their knees and those that were lying down rose up on their knees and there they stayed kneeling and moaning, the tears running down their faces.' "

Francis Kilvert

85

God bless the master of this house,
And the good missis too.
And all the little children
That about the table go.
I wish you a merry Christmas
And a happy New Year,
A good fat pig in the larder
To last you all year.

Traditional

If Christmas Day on Thursday be,
A windy winter you shall see,
Windy weather in each week,
And hard tempests strong and thick,
The summer shall be good and dry,
Corn and beasts shall multiply.

Traditional

BIRDS AT WINTER NIGHTFALL

Around the house the flakes fly faster,
And all the berries now are gone
From holly and cotonea-aster
Around the house. The flakes fly! – faster
Shutting indoors that crumb-outcaster
We used to see upon the lawn
Around the house. The flakes fly faster,
And all the berries now are gone!

Thomas Hardy

If New Year's Eve night wind blow south,
It betokeneth warmth and growth:
If west, much milk, and fish in the sea:
If north, much cold, and storms there will be:
If east, the trees will bear much fruit:
If north-east, flee it man and brute.

Traditional

Candlemas is February 2nd.

If Candlemas day be sunny and bright
Winter will have another flight.
But if Candlemas day be clouds and rain,
Winter is gone and will not come again.

Traditional

The sun, which quite forsakes the upper walk of the new garden about the end of October, begins now to shine full along it about half an hour before it sets. The Hepaticas, Crocuss, snowdrops & double daisies begin now to make a very agreeable appearance as the first promise of spring. Warm moist weather, which makes the grass spring sensibly.

Gilbert White

Larks soaring and singing the first time; one to an immense height; rain in morning, afternoon mild but a strong wind from west; catkins on hazel, and buds on some hazel-bushes; missel-thrush singing in copse; spring seems to have burst on us all at once; chaffinches pairing, or trying to; fighting.

Richard Jefferies

CHILDREN'S SONG ON VALENTINE'S DAY

Mornty, mornty, Valentine!
Blow the oats against the wind,
We are ragged and you are fine,
So please to give us a Valentine.

Traditional

Sad wintry weather; a north-east wind; a sun that puts out one's eyes, without affording the slightest warmth; dryness that chaps lips and hands like a frost in December; rain that comes chilling and arrowy like hail in January; nature at a dead pause; no seeds up in the garden; no leaves out in the hedgerows; no cowslips swinging their pretty bells in the fields; no nightingales in the dingles; no swallows skimming round the great pond; no cuckoos (that ever I should miss that rascally sonneteer) in any part! Nevertheless there is something of a charm in this wintery spring, this putting back of the seasons. If the flower-clock must stand still for a month or two, could it choose a better time than that of the primroses and violets?

Mary Russell Mitford

Oh, Adam was a gardener, and God who made him sees
That half a proper gardener's work is done upon his knees,
So when your work is finished, you can wash your hands and
     pray
For the Glory of the Garden, that it may not pass away!
And the Glory of the Garden it shall never pass away!

Rudyard Kipling

If you would be happy for a week take a wife,
If you would be happy for a month kill a pig,
But if you would be happy all your life plant a garden.

Traditional

THE OAK

Live thy life,
    Young and old,
Like yon oak,
Bright in spring,
    Living gold;

Summer-rich
    Then; and then
Autumn-changed,
Soberer-hued
    Gold again.

Alfred, Lord Tennyson

If Winter comes, can Spring be far behind?

Percy Bysshe Shelley